FOUNDATION BUILDING CAMPAIGN

Second Edition

MICHAEL L. STICKLER

THE VisionGROUP LTD

Foundation Building Campaign
Second Edition
By Michael L. Stickler

Additional copies and other resources available at: MikeStickler.com.

Printed in the United States of America.

ISBN: 9780990744139

Editor:
Mariah Bliss
Compass Communications, LLC.

Publisher:
The Vision Group, Ltd.
www.thevisiongroupltd.com

Dear Reader:

Congratulations – you've just picked up your copy of **Foundation Building Campaign**.

Many nonprofit leaders struggle to understand why they're not raising as many funds as they could be. God has given them a vision – but they're having a hard time turning that vision into reality. That's why I'm especially excited that you've downloaded **Foundation Building Campaign**. It's not a cookie-cutter boilerplate book with information you've seen thousands of times.

Instead, you'll find time-tested strategies, powerful techniques, and "a-ha!" realizations that make all the difference in taking your fundraising efforts to the next level.

Try these out for yourself, and see how God's vision for your nonprofit foundation blossoms and grows.

As always, share your feedback with me at MikeStickler.com.

Thank you!

Mike Stickler

FOUNDATION BUILDING CAMPAIGN
TABLE OF CONTENTS

TABLE OF CONTENTS continued...

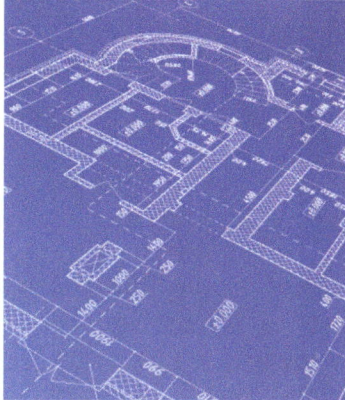

INTRODUCTION

Nonprofit organizations have a passion to help people. Nonprofit leaders and managers work hard to make a difference in the lives of their clients. Whether they provide social services, like counseling or mentoring; a product, like food or housing; or spiritual nutriment, the goal of a nonprofit is to positively impact the lives of others.

Because of this desire, nonprofits attempt to use their resources wisely. Pouring time, effort, and money into people is the organization's ultimate passion or reason for existence. Sometimes, however, the nonprofit organization is the one that needs help. The organization may need to improve its own foundation before helping other people stand on theirs. It is difficult to run an efficient operation without the proper infrastructure — facilities that will support the mission of the organization.

Funding a building is always challenging. After pouring the organization's funds into people, there may not be enough remaining in the budget to pay for the monthly bills, let alone build a building. What should an organization do? That is where we can help. The desire for this book and the accompanying workshop is to give you enough information to make intelligent decisions about how your organization can raise the funds necessary to meet your infrastructure needs without negatively impacting the work you are passionately doing.

In the Wizard of Oz, Dorothy finds herself in a strange place, longing for home. In order to get back to her home in Kansas, Dorothy is forced to journey to the Emerald City and seek out the wizard. The story of her adventures in the journey to Oz will provide a framework for this discussion.

BIBLICAL PRINCIPLES OF FUND RAISING

1. Proportionate Giving

Nowhere in the Bible does it ever suggest that you take the need, divide it by the number of households and ask everyone for the same amount. Instead, we are taught proportionate giving. When Moses was raising funds to build the tabernacle (Exodus 35) he asked the people for an offering. We are told that some brought gold, some silver, some wood. Each one responded as they had been blessed.

2. Over and Above Giving

(I Chronicles 29): King David wanted to build the new temple in Jerusalem. But God said, "No." David was a warrior king and God wanted Solomon to build the temple. Instead of sulking (as I might have done), David decided that if he could not build it, he would raise the funds for Solomon. David starts by calling the leadership of the nation together. He told them that out of their regular tithes and offerings money had been set aside for construction of the new temple, but it was not enough. They needed more. He asked for an offering, 'over and above' what they were already giving (phrase found in New American Standard Bible). It does not do the organization any good if people simply divert what they are already giving. We are asking for new money, over and above.

3. Leadership Leads

(I Chronicles 29): Then David tells the leadership what he is giving and asks them to give. They respond generously. A huge amount is committed. The news goes throughout the land and the people rejoice. Then they *start* giving. Leadership needs to lead. They need to be the first to make their commitments.

4. Sacrificial Giving

(Mark 12:41-44): A woman is giving her two copper coins to the temple offering. God has sacrificed so much for us in the giving of His Son for us. He obviously notices and is pleased when we sacrifice back to him.

5. Prayer First

(II Corinthians 8:5): Paul was collecting money for the church in Jerusalem. In speaking of the Macedonian churches he says "they did not do as we expected. They gave themselves first to the Lord and then to us in keeping with His will." In other words, they prayed first.

These are the principles upon which this program is built. It is also more than just theory and philosophy. We believe that a capital stewardship campaign should be more than just a financial journey, it should be a spiritual journey.

If all we did was announce that on this date we were going to have a commitment time for the project (if anyone came), all we would get would be surplus money – pocket change. People would make financial decisions based on what is in their bank account.

We need to help people understand that this is a faith-based financial decision. We need to take them on a spiritual journey of faith that culminates in a sacrifical, proportionate, and over and above financial commitment. *How do we do that?* We invite them to join the journey by:

> **1. Involving them.** If you can get 20 people to do your calling for an event, do it. Even if you have 2 dedicated people who offer to handle it. Involvement starts people on the journey.
>
> **2. Informing them.** People need information. They need it in many forms, many times. Go overboard with communication.
>
> **3. Calling them to pray.** Individual and corporate prayer will make a difference.
>
> **4. Inspiring them to give.** Inspire them with:
> - Your vision and the case
> - Stewardship education – devotional and teaching materials
> - Include children and youth

If you can get people to pray "Lord, what you do want to do through me to meet this need," then we win. Now it is up to God to direct them to the commitment he wants them to make. We don't have to pressure anyone. *This thing is about prayer, not pressure.*

Chapter One: There is No Place Like Home... Visioneering

Ultimately, Dorothy wanted to go home to Kansas. That desire was her vision. Everything she did was in a purposeful attempt to get her back to Kansas. Organizations need a solid vision and mission to know where they are attempting to go.

Chapter Two: We're Off to See the Wizard... Developing the Case for Your Project

What was the purpose of the Emerald City? Dorothy learned that the only way to get home was to see the Wizard in Emerald City. Organizations need to be able to clearly define how the campaign will help to accomplish their vision.

Chapter Three: The Scarecrow, The Tin Man, and The Cowardly Lion... Sources of Funding

Along the journey, Dorothy recruited three companions. As a team, they made a journey that none of them could have complete alone. Organizations need help to embark upon a capital journey. As others begin to comprehend the trip, they will learn about the benefits (to themselves, to the community and to the organization) of becoming funding partners.

Chapter Four: The Ruby Slippers... Developing a Communication Strategy

Dorothy was instructed never to remove her slippers. This was a way to communicate a message to her friends and enemies. Organizations need to develop their own slippers in the form of a communication strategy.

Chapter Five: The Yellow Brick Road... Beginning the Journey

"Following the Yellow Brick Road" was the key to keeping Dorothy focused on the task at hand. If organizations are to achieve their capital dreams, they will need to clearly define their own progressive paths.

We're off...

CHAPTER ONE:

THERE IS NO PLACE LIKE HOME... VISIONEERING

Why are you here?

Most likely, every participant in this seminar is a leader with a heart for his or her ministry. Suppose all of you have a desire to further your ministries by partaking in a building campaign. Do you know how having a vision can propel your organization? Have you already learned how to develop realistic foresight? Do you want to dream accessible goals? Do you desire greater things for your organization than what you can currently imagine?

If I had to guess, I'd say you all want to follow the Lord's leading in your ministries. You want to be true to His Word, unlike the prophets of Samaria who, "speak visions from their own minds, not from the mouth of the Lord" (Jeremiah 23:16). During this seminar, you will learn to discern whether or not you're leading from the Straight and True. When you say, "The Lord is leading us…" you will speak with integrity (Ezekiel 13: 6-9).

The Lord said through his prophet Joel, "Your sons and daughters will prophesy, your old men will dream dreams, your young men will see visions" (Joel 2:28). In other words, by maintaining a vision for your organization, you are seeking the Lord and maintaining your youth!

According to bestselling author Andy Stanley, visioneering is "a clear mental picture of what could be, fueled by the conviction that it should be."[1] In this seminar, we'll learn what a vision is, how a vision comes to be, how to make your vision a reality, how to know it's real, and how the vision can take your ministry to its ultimate destination. Before we delve into the creation of a vision, however, let's discuss the larger picture: the four key components (including vision) that define our organization's purpose.

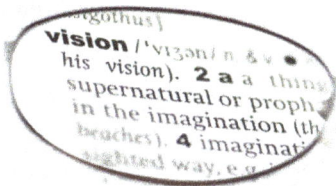

VISION, MISSION, VALUES AND GOALS: FOCUS, FOCUS, FOCUS

Too many people and organizations try to be all things, in all places, at all times. That only works in the movies. The reality is that, like an athlete, people and organizations are most effective when they're focused on a goal and a target. While many people think they know their goals and targets, they often squirm when you push them for details. They can only offer vague, overly broad statements. Clearly defining your vision, mission, values and goals (VMVGs) can take time, but it can also bring incredible focus and relief to an entire organization. Why? Because leaders finally understand their target, which means they can ignore everything else without guilt.

Each of the four aspects of your philosophy are distinctly different. Understanding the differences can help you better define what, when, why, and how you're accomplishing your goals. Clearly defined VMVGs can help you prioritize tasks, eliminate distractions and fast-track valuable opportunities. Please, please, please… do NOT confuse any of the four statements with a catchy marketing phrase. Marketing phrases are temporary ways to communicate your philosophy based on the trends of your target market. Vision, mission, values and goals will define your organization and become part of its identity.

Vision

Vision is the biggest of the big pictures. Your vision is the grandest accomplishment you can imagine. Be careful not to set an impossible mark, as it may discourage or depress you. Here are some sample vision statements which may illustrate the concept. The vision of The Vision Group (TVG) is "to see God's Kingdom advanced." One of our employee's personal life vision is "to share the joy of an eternal relationship with God with new believers." When trying to make a good decision, or when push comes to shove or a situation feels confusing, our company and our employees can ask themselves "Will this help us/me achieve the vision?" It's amazing how often that question produces a quick and confident answer. A strong vision sells itself.

Mission

Now, on to your mission; this is how you can achieve your vision. Our mission is "to connect God's people with the resources needed to build strong foundations and realize their dreams." Okay, that's a bit on the long side (in our opinion) but it says what's in our hearts. Our employees' mission is "to encourage, educate, and evangelize." Some might think that's too vague a statement, but our employees likes the flexibility it offers.

Values

Your values are the guardrails of life. Values help keep you on the straight and narrow. Here's an example: Our employees' values are "faith, hope, and love." This means that everything said and done should convey or support faith in God, hope for the future, and love for self and others. If those three values are missing from something said or done, it's time to make a correction.

Goals

Lastly, your goals are the specific objectives you wish to achieve. Unfortunately, most people (and companies) confuse their goals with their mission. One way to clarify the situation is to remember that a good goal will meet all of the following criteria:

1. A goal must have a clearly defined objective.
2. A goal must have action steps.
3. A goal must have timelines.
4. A goal must be written.
5. A goal must have the ability to be easily presented to someone (like a foundation).

By meeting these criteria, you ensure that your staff, volunteers, clients and donors know what you want to achieve. Each participant will know their assigned portion of the project (action steps) and how long they can work on it (timelines). Writing the goal forces you to put your idea into words. It also gives you and others a chance to look at it and ask, "Does this make sense?" Finally, you must be able to clearly present the goal to someone who knows nothing about your organization, your vision or your clients. You should be able to do this in two written sentences or ten verbal seconds.

A bad example of a goal would be something like, "I want to help poor kids be safe, healthy, and happy." That sounds more like a mission statement because the need for all three objectives will exist forever.

A better example would be, "My organization wants to improve literacy rates among low-income youth in our city. We plan to do this by increasing reading scores 50% amongst 3rd and 4th graders through a weekly mentoring program at City Elementary School during the 2014-2015 school year."

Here's a quick list (some real, some imagined) to get your mental wheels spinning:

Group: Ford Motor Company
Vision: To become the #1 auto seller in the world
Mission: Quality is Job 1
Goal: Sales Targets

Group: Thompson Publishing
Vision: To become the #1 supplier of legal information materials
Mission: Quality, Service, Price
Goal: Sales Targets

Group: Pro Football Team
Vision: To become the NFL's dominant team
Mission: Win more games and set more records than any other team
Values: Hard work, focus, determination
Goals: Championships at all levels (division, conference, and league)

Christian organizations often pick a Bible verse for one or more of their VMVGs. There's nothing wrong with that approach if the verse is an appropriate match, but don't pick a verse to impress God or other people. God doesn't care how you word it, and other people (especially non-Christians) might not understand what you're trying to communicate. By carefully picking your words and keeping each statement as brief as possible, you'll be able to craft phrases which are easy to remember, easy to say, and have impact when shared via conversation or print.

Once you've clarified your VMVGs, share them. Share them everywhere and with everybody, both inside and outside your NPO. Print them on your business cards, letterhead, brochures, etc. Hang banners in your office. Print them on sheets of paper, frame them, and have them hanging by everyone's desk or phone. These are so fundamentally important that they need to become an ingrained part of your NPO. Everything you do, think, say and decide should support and reflect your VMVG.

One final thought: entire books have been written on VMVGs and how you should go about creating and implementing them. The bottom line is that it'll take a lot of time, energy, and input from your co-workers, family and friends (i.e. "Hey, does this make sense to you?"). Be patient and let the Holy Spirit shape the creation process.

DEVELOPING YOUR
VISION, MISSION, VALUES AND GOALS

Ask yourself these questions to determine your VMVGs:

Vision: What's the grandest accomplishment I can imagine for my ministry?

_____
_____
_____
_____

Mission: What major method(s) will I use to achieve these lofty dreams?

_____
_____
_____
_____

Values: What core principles / morals / ideals are uncompromisingly important to me?

_____
_____
_____
_____

Goals: What specific objective(s) do I wish to achieve?

_____
_____
_____

WHAT IS VISION?

Vision is the correct pair of glasses: through them you see the future clearly.

According to Darrell Young and Joseph Hester, "Visions are passions that evoke emotions, motivation where the mundane begins to matter, directions that become a moral compass, and purpose, which gives meaning to life."[2] Visions add a purpose to an organization. "Work without purpose (even if it takes great skill) can become mindless, heartless drudgery. Add purpose, even to so-called grunt work, and our work lives take on an expanded, inspired dimension."[3]

Your vision is the greatest accomplishment you can imagine. It shapes everything you do and is the broadest way to define your organization. Organizational leaders with "a clear vision invent excellent futures for their companies; those who lack it set their companies adrift in dangerous waters."[4] Where is your organization's vision? Where is your personal vision?

"There is no more powerful engine driving an organization toward excellence and long-range success than an attractive, worthwhile, and achievable vision of the future, [that is] widely shared."[5]

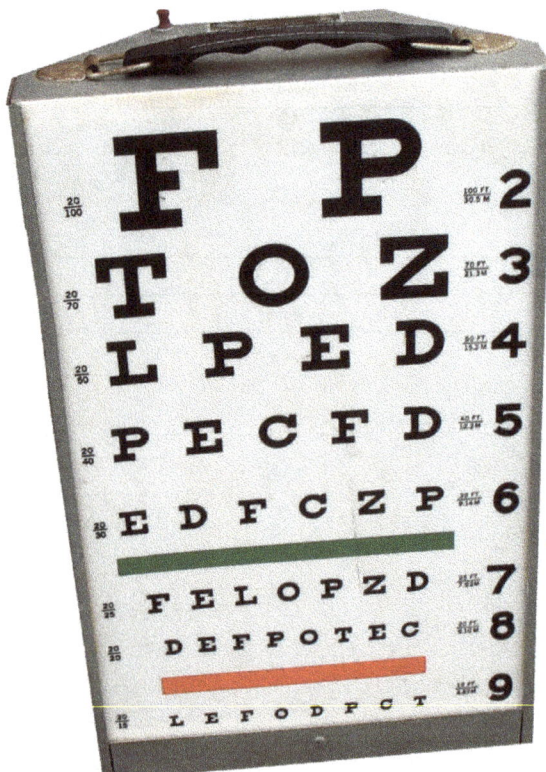

For example, the vision of The Vision Group, Ltd., is, "to see God's kingdom advanced." Another ministry's vision may be "to end homelessness in our county," or "to end racial prejudice in the inner city," or simply, "to disciple twentysomethings into a growing relationship with Christ." Notice that these vision statements are very short—only one sentence long, action-oriented, and easy to remember.

If a ministry ever gets into a confusing situation, the board members and staff can ask themselves, "Will this help us achieve the vision?" The vision helps to provide clarity and is invaluable in recruiting supporters. "Leaders energize through generating and sustaining creative tension, through fostering commitment to realizing a dream and to telling the truth about what is."[6] A strong vision sells itself. Strong visions "provide people with an image of what can be and [motivates] them to move ahead into the future they envision."[7]

Visionaries are often misunderstood because:

1. They seem compulsive. Often visionaries live in the future, rather than in the here and now, to create lasting prospects.

2. They appear to have a "multi-level marketing attitude." How many times have you heard something like this: "Listen, if we can just get people on board with our vision, then we can really get somewhere!"

3. Everything they say and do is through the "lens" of their vision. Try putting on someone else's glasses and looking at the world. It is pretty difficult, isn't it?

4. They do not clearly communicate their vision to others. They often do not have the "skills of influencing people to enthusiastically work toward goals identified as being for the common good, with character that inspires confidence."[8] Bad communication or breaks in communication are the leading cause of misunderstandings.[9]

Fact: "In a survey of 1,500 senior leaders from 20 countries, 98 percent of them said that the most important behavior trait needed of leaders was a strong sense of vision."[10]

THE BIRTH OF THE VISION

How does a vision come to be? What are the steps to creating a vision that is intentional and effective in nature? Tichy and Devanna say that the organization needs to frame the problem, collect data on the problem and dumb the problem down. By doing this, the leaders will be able to set the mindset of the organization in a direction of visioneering.[11] John P. Kotter, the Konosuke Matsushita Professor of Leadership at Harvard's Business School, came up with the following steps to create an effective vision:

• **First draft:** The process often starts with an initial statement from a single individual, reflecting both his/her dreams and real marketplace needs.

• **Role of the guiding coalition:** The first draft is always modeled over time by the guiding coalition or an even larger group of people. In other words, have the board of directors look over the draft.

• **Importance of teamwork:** The group process never works well without a minimum of effective teamwork.

• **Role of the head and the heart:** Both analytical thinking and a lot of dreaming are essential throughout the activity.

• **Messiness of the process:** Vision creation is usually a process of two steps forward and one back, movement to the left and then to the right.

• **Time frame:** Vision is never created in a single meeting. The activity takes months, sometimes years.

• **End product:** The process results in a direction for the future that is desirable, feasible, focused, flexible, and is conveyable in [one cogent sentence].[12]

Creating a vision can begin with several sources—a personal experience that creates an intentional empathy, an internal urgency to meet a need, or an external calling for someone to act in a certain way.

Personal experience creates intentional empathy

A vision often stems from a personal experience or burden that God has placed on your heart. The Apostle Paul spent a large portion of his adulthood persecuting Christians and the Church. When he had a personal encounter with Jesus on his way to Damascus (Acts 9), it changed his pattern of thought. Whether a vision is formed through personal experience or through a heavenly burden, that vision will create an intentional empathy within you toward those in need. Whether your vision is to help the homeless in your community, minister to the teenagers in your neighborhood or travel to third world countries to preach the Gospel, your desire to help those in need will increase as your vision grows. An emotional attachment will develop. A vision is something that gets into your heart and penetrates your spirit.

You will feel an urgency to meet a need

A vision is also a picture of something that has not happened yet and about a need that has to be met. In 1 Kings 17, Elijah, a prophet of God, was confronted with the death of a widow's son. She had fed him previously even though she and her son had nothing, so this was not the first meeting between the two. Elijah was confronted with this crisis and felt an urgency to meet the widow's need. All great leaders recognize the needs of others and seek to meet them. "The focus of servant-leadership is on sharing information, building a common vision, self-management, high levels of interdependence, learning from mistakes, encouraging creative input from every team member, and questioning present assumptions and mental models."[13] True servant-leaders should never lose track of other people's needs. It is the passion to meet those needs that will drive your vision and keep you on the right path towards achieving your goals. Here are five steps to practicing servant-leadership in the organization to help birth the mission:

1. Listen without judgment
2. Be authentic
3. Build community
4. Share power
5. Develop people[14]

You see an external cry for action

Visions can sometimes begin due to an external force, like Pat Tillman who was a National Football League star with a 3.6 million contract to play for the Arizona Cardinals. In the wake of September 11, he saw the need for troops and joined the Army Rangers. In 2004, he was killed in friendly fire.

In the Old Testament, Moses was born into a doomed life, yet rescued into a life of luxury. After growing up in the Pharaoh's palace, he saw an Egyptian treating another Hebrew badly and reacted (Exodus 2:11-15). Leaders of organizations need to be both proactive and reactive in the formation of their visions. They need to ensure that the "vision honors the past, is a significant tool for managing change, is the essence of effective leadership, and is the single most important motivator of people."[15]

VISION DEVELOPMENT MATRIX

At the cornerstone of every ministry and organization should be the Vision Development Matrix, a guideline that demonstrates how to share your vision with others. It is based on the principle that raising time and money is not about manipulation; it's about building relationships based on your vision. It's also important to remember that money is not the only goal. Time is often more of a sacrificial gift than finances, so please encourage your donors to give of themselves in this way as well. The steps below will help you share your vision and then reap the benefits of fruitful donor development.

VISION	DEVELOPMENT
Own It How can I...	Parnter Heart of, How can I...
Catch It Ask questions	Constituent Sacrificial Gift
See It Touch it, Feel it, Smell it	Donor Pocket Change
Hear It Introduced to it for the first time	Prospects Never heard your vision

VISION SHARING STAGES:

1. **Hear It.** Your first task is to share the vision with friends and potential donors. Since they're being introduced to it for the first time, communicate it simply through your newsletter, website, or a conversation. Take them to lunch and tell them what you do and why you're passionate about it. This step is designed to be simple and relational.

2. **See It.** The second step is to invite the friend or donor to see the vision. Encourage them to visit the facility, or invite them to a gathering where they can meet the people you help. For example, if you run a homeless shelter, invite one or two of the homeless men to join you so they can be introduced. You want them to touch, feel and smell the vision for themselves.

3. **Catch It.** In this stage of understanding, the donor's imagination will be employed. Because you've already told them about the vision and they've experienced it for themselves, they begin to ask questions and participate directly in the vision.

4. **Own It.** Finally, the donor is totally involved in the vision of your organization. Their attitude is one of complete dedication. You won't have to ask them to volunteer or to give, because their natural response is, "How can I help?" The "own it" stage is exactly where you want all of your supporters.

THE POWER TO MAKE YOUR VISION A REALITY

How do you know you have a vision?

1. **You know you have a vision when it sticks.** There is an instinctive bonding that goes on between you and those you want to help, and it sticks with you wherever you go. If you cannot stop thinking about it or praying about it, you probably have a vision. Remember that everyone is unique with different talents and gifts, so it only makes sense that certain things stick with you and others do not. God wired you in a particular way to carry certain burdens while letting other people carry other burdens. If it doesn't stick to you, let someone else do it!

2. **You know you have a vision when you develop an intensifying burden for the need.** Beyond just the feeling of wanting to help, a vision will get into your spirit and create a growing burden for those in need. Do not move forward without the burden from God, and always stop to pray and discover God's heart about the need. It is easy to get ahead of yourself and place yourself in front of God.

3. **You know you have a vision when you have an intuitive belief that you can meet the need.** A vision that comes from God is overwhelming. There are likely many steps and aspects to the vision that will need to be addressed, and it may seem impossible at first. But ours is a God of the impossible, and if a vision is from the Lord, he will pave the way. A vision will create a feeling in your spirit that says, "I don't know *how* to do it, but know I *need* to do it."

4. **You know you have a vision when you have an internal accountability for the need.** Will you accept the responsibility to make it happen? If your answer is "yes," then you are well on your way. Your vision is probably not working just yet, but if it is still in your heart and spirit, it becomes a matter of will A vision will take time, effort, grace, and lots of prayer; but when your vision is strong, the hard work becomes secondary to your conviction to meet the need.

The following list of properties of transforming visions
is adapted from Burt Nanus' book Visionary Leadership:

- They fit the organization in the here and now.

- They set the standard extremely high, yet are attainable in the near future.

- They clarify the direction and the purpose of the organization.

- They inspire those within the organization to excellence.

- They are articulated well and understood.

- They display the uniqueness of the organization.

- They are ambitious.[16]

Visions are individual to the company and are validated through the input of all involved personnel. Visions are "farsighted (they see the big picture in developing a vision for the future); enterprising (they enjoy taking on new projects and programs); persuasive (they present new ideas in ways that create buy-in); [and] resourceful (they use existing resources to create successful new ventures)."[17]

What a vision is NOT:

1. Vision does not surrender individual dreams. Many times, the members of the organization will interpret a vision as a forced goal. Ultimately, "when you ask people to do something different, they focus on what they have to give up, not on what they are going to gain."[18] Visioneering is an attempt to get everyone on the same page, but everyone may not interpret it as such. For this reason, it is important to reiterate the organization's new vision time and time again and keep the dialog open between the organization and its stakeholders.[19]

2. Vision is not a prophecy for the organization. The vision of the organization is an ideal for the future. It is "a futuristic design for its progression to accomplish goals and dreams."[20] When a vision becomes reality, it does so because of the way the organization captures other's imaginations, mobilizes resources, and reshapes the reality at hand.[21]

3. Vision is not a static statement. It "relies on actions to bring the image of the future to fruition."[22] When formatting a vision, the organization should see that formulation is "a dynamic process, an integral part of the ongoing task of visionary leadership."[23]

4. Vision is neither true nor false. "It can be evaluated only relative to other possible directions for the organization. That is, it can be seen as better or worse, more or less rational, safer or riskier, more or less appropriate or even just good enough."[24]

"Where there is no vision, the people perish."
—*Proverbs 29:18*

THE TESTS OF THE VISION

After you experience the burden and confirm your vision, it is your job to take the first step in making it happen. Become an expert in the field, be proactive, and put in your due diligence. "When the vision is stated as a specific destination with a specific date of arrival, decision making becomes easier for everyone in the company. The vision not only clarifies what the company is trying to become; it also states what the company is trying not to become. A clear vision minimizes the likelihood the company will be seduced by short-term opportunities."[26] After that, just sit back and watch as your vision flourishes under the hand of the Lord.

If you experience ridicule for your vision, then you're not so different from many other recipients of God's call, including Joseph (Genesis 37:5-11). Even when he was mocked for his seeming dreams of grandeur, he believed that God has placed the vision in his heart for a purpose and did not give up faith. It is important to remember that "every remarkable artistic achievement starts as nothing more than a dream, usually of one individual, and not infrequently contested and ridiculed by friends and colleagues. Such a vision is not much different from one a leader develops for an organization, for leadership itself is also an art form…The best visionary leaders, like the best artists, are always seeking to communicate directly and viscerally a vision of the world that will resonate with the deepest meanings of people and cause them to embrace it as worthwhile and elevating."[27]

Here are some questions to ask yourself. Remember to answer as honestly as possible. Don't feel bad if you haven't found your vision yet.

What are the needs of others? _____
_____
_____
_____

What are the needs in my community? _____
_____
_____
_____

How do I know what these needs are? _____
_____
_____
_____

Am I truly motivated by the needs of my community (or do other motives exist)? _____
_____
_____
_____

Should I do something about these needs? _____
_____
_____
_____

Should I teach about the needs? _____
_____
_____

Am I wired to meet these needs? In what ways? _____
_____
_____

Has God uniquely positioned me in my community to meet these needs? How? _____
_____
_____

Do I believe I have the ability to meet these needs? In what ways? _____
_____
_____

Do I feel accountable to this need? _____
_____
_____
_____

Is my vision stuck on me? Why do I think this? _____
_____
_____
_____

Am I willing to take the first step and start the vision? _____
_____
_____
_____

In what ways have I put in my due diligence? _____
_____
_____
_____

In what ways have I shown perseverance in my vision? _____
_____
_____
_____

Is my spouse in agreement? Why or why not? _____
_____
_____
_____

Remember: Hope is not a strategy!

"The eyes of the Lord are on those who fear Him, on those whose hope is in His unfailing love…We wait in hope for the Lord; He is our help and our shield. In Him our hearts rejoice, for we trust in His holy name. May your unfailing love rest upon us, O Lord, even as we put our hope in you."

—Psalm 33:18, 20-22

CHAPTER TWO:
WE'RE OFF TO SEE THE WIZARD...
DEVELOPING THE CASE FOR YOUR PROJECT

After clearly defining the vision, mission, values, and goals of an organization, individuals need to begin to plan how to turn that vision into reality. After all, a vision without a plan is really just a dream. Now is the time to begin to put feet to the vision.

In the same way that Dorothy knew she wanted to go home to Kansas, most organizations have a pretty good idea about the place that they want to go. Similar to Dorothy's knowledge about the general goal to get her home (seeing the wizard), most organizations realize that some kind of physical plant addition, renovation, and/or building is necessary. If this is the realization, organizations need to find a way to communicate to others how this building program is going to help the organization accomplish its vision. This chapter will explain the process for developing a compelling "case" for any capital project – a reason for people to give sacrificially. Without a compelling case, most organizations will be given plenty of nice head nods but very little principle. Consider the following story:

Pastor Denny's church had relocated a decade ago with a nice building, but it never grew. The congregation would jump to between 200-210 people in attendance, but it would ultimately drop back down to 160. This pattern was repeated three separate times over the last 20 years. The pastor had a heart for evangelism that was outward evidence of an internal gift. People came to believe in Jesus Christ as a result of his preaching, but the church never reflected that growth. The vision was in place, but progress was lacking.

Some individuals began to ask, "Why aren't we growing?" Some thought the problem stemmed from the church's location, its chosen worship style, or maybe even the senior pastor. Pastor Denny was convinced that the issue was parking. The church sanctuary sat 350, but the location only had on-site parking for 43 cars. Curbside parking was available for another 43 cars, but this only brought the total to 96 parking spots (if the local neighbors were not entertaining that weekend). Denny figured that it was the limit of 96 parking spots that stunted the church's growth. To his knowledge, the answer was simple—finding more parking would alleviate the problem! In some places, additional parking would be an easy fix, but not in the outskirts of New York City. The price of land was atrocious! Denny calculated that filling the auditorium with 350 people would require an additional 67 parking spots. This calculation was done with the assumption that each parking spot held one car that brought 2.15 people to church. To buy enough land for 67 parking spots was going to cost the church almost $700,000. To get the spaces, they would have to purchase two local houses, tear them down, and pave the lots. How does anyone, let alone an evangelistic minister in the suburbs of New York City, make a compelling case that will motivate people into giving $700,000 for 67 parking spaces?

The way that Pastor Denny developed his case was interesting. He calculated it thusly: Every new parking spot will bring 2.15 new souls into the Kingdom of God. Each new parking spot would cost $10,000. Investing $10,000 to see a return of 2.15 people come to Christ yields an excellent ROI. The membership caught the evangelistic vision. They understood the link between parking spots and expanding the Kingdom; therefore, they funded the program. Presently they have completed the first phase (15 new parking spots), and the attendance has risen by an average of 30 individuals per week! People are excited to pay for more parking because they caught the vision.

It is absolutely crucial to link the vision and mission of your organization with your building plan. Better yet, make sure to have a separate yet similar vision and mission for your building plan that helps you to fulfill the organization's vision and mission! People need to know what the organization is attempting to do and what it will cost. Before they give, they want to know why they should give. They want to know what kind of difference this campaign will make to the future of the organization in its quest to fulfill its vision and mission.

DEVELOPING A COMPELLING CASE

Developing a compelling case always begins by assessing the need of an organization. Finding out the truth behind an organization's needs will help in determining if the organization is heading in the correct direction. When assessing the need, take the time to sit down and make a detailed list of all the things that a Foundation Building Campaign could fund for your organization. After listing all of those things, assign a priority to them from 1-99, if you have 99 funding desires. If at all possible, make sure to do this exercise with other leaders in your organization. Remember that two heads are always better than one! Ensure that the group reaches a consensus on how to determine the priority of the needs. State the cost(s) or estimated cost(s) involved in fulfilling the needs. Finally, brainstorm about all of the possible ways that a successful campaign will make a difference in the lives of the people you serve.

Organizational Needs

Before going any further, take some time to answer some questions:

Why are we thinking about doing this project/these projects? _____
_____
_____
_____

What makes this project important? _____
_____
_____
_____

Why do we need to do this now? Can it not wait for five more years? _____
_____
_____
_____

What specific programs do we offer that will be positively impacted by this project? _____
_____
_____
_____

What are our specific financial needs?_____
_____
_____
_____

WHY should the organization's stakeholders support the organization? _____
_____
_____
_____

How will this campaign specifically benefit the stakeholders and the organization? _____
_____
_____
_____

Tip: When formulating a mission statement for your campaign, remember that it will be very easy for the writer to assume that everyone understands the needs being addressed in the statement. The writer needs to put himself or herself into the place of the reader. In short, ALWAYS think of what you are writing, and remember to ask, "Why should the reader care about this?"

The Initial Writing

Good writing will cause a chain reaction for the readers. Good writing will grab the reader's attention. To do so, expose the problem or need in the first line of the first paragraph. Use a picture, an authoritative quotation, a question, or another attention-getting device. Make sure to create some interest in the statement to cause the reader to desire to learn more. Whenever writing, make sure to convey the confidence that you want people to know that you have. If you don't believe in what you are trying to say, why are you trying to say it? Make sure that the plan is clear and simple—the opportunity is at hand, and this is the time and place to perform the capital campaign. Realize that simply sharing the vision will bring people along, but getting people to catch it and own the vision will create an intrinsic desire for the stakeholders to do something personal in the process. Finally, call the people to action. Make it clear to the readers what they can do to help and why they should do it immediately.

Keys to a Compelling Case

There are seven main keys that help to create a compelling case. These are:

1. Let your words paint pictures in the minds of the readers.

2. Avoid using long, difficult words and jargon. (These merely cause people to focus on trying to understand the meaning of a word, or they will simply skim over a possibly crucial sentence or paragraph.)

3. Be careful with your use of language. Remember the audience, and communicate with them.

4. Use phrases that transition your writing to help it flow. Phrases like "as a result," "in light of," or "therefore" are wonderful words that force readers to tie in the latter with the former.

5. Promise programs, not desperate plights. People want to be assistants in success. They do not want to give to a discouraging or dying organization.

6. Remember that people are interested in people. Use personal stories and testimonies whenever and wherever possible.

7. Be optimistic, enthusiastic, challenging, and promising in your use of words.

Components to a Compelling Case:

A compelling case needs to be written clearly, concisely, and completely. Overall, there are five main ingredients to a compelling case:

1. Start with your history. In one paragraph, explain how the ministry has expanded due to the work of God.

2. State your vision. Clearly articulate how past events lead up to the present time. Then show how the present will lead the organization into the foreseeable future.

3. Introduce the need and the timelines. Explain that in order to get from Point A to Point B, the organization needs to do this project. Explain why and how long is needed to be successful.

4. Unveil the solution and its benefits. Introduce the need for raising funds by explaining the path of fundraising chosen for the project and the benefits of a solid plan of action.

5. Close it up. Remember to tie it all back to the organization's mission and vision statements.

It is crucial that the case be compelling, but it is also crucial to be concise. If at all possible, keep this portion limited to 1-2 pages. In it, you should attempt to honor the past, look to the future, articulate the need, show the plan for success and ask for support.

GOING FARTHER

Have you ever wondered why your seatbacks and tray tables need to be in their "upright and locked position" upon the takeoff and landing of any commercial aircraft? It is not just because the head flight attendants love to say those words. Those portions of the flight are the most dangerous, for it is during those times that runway incursions can occur.

> "A runway incursion is any occurrence at an airport involving an aircraft, vehicle, person, or object on the ground that creates a collision hazard or results in a loss of separation…This separation loss can happen to a departing aircraft, or one preparing for a takeoff. Planes that are landing or intending to land can become subject to a loss of separation or incursion…Ground operations are fertile ground for incursions."[28]

Building campaigns should not necessarily proceed just because they have been given the go-ahead by all internal personnel. Just like a pilot needs to know when to abort a landing or takeoff due to a runway incursion, you need to know when to abort or modify the building campaign due to an obstacle in the road ahead. "Leadership, in part, is the capacity to adapt quickly to a changing environment."[29]

So far, this book has addressed the development of a solid vision statement, the determination of whether the organization is ready for such a large step, and building the case statement. Now it is time to display ways to discern God's will for the campaign, teach you how to raise the support of others, and assess the ministry's potential for development.

HOW TO KNOW IF THE BUILDING CAMPAIGN IS GOD'S WILL

Is your desire to grow into a new building given to you by God, or is the "moving of the Spirit" the result of some bad tacos? Here are five biblical ways to discern the will of God:

1. Scripture: God's Word is infallible and inspired by the Holy Spirit (2 Timothy 3:16). As you study the Bible, do you see Him speaking on the issue, or is He silent? If He does address the issue, is your vision in step with His, or are you trying to add something to the Scriptures (Revelation 22:18-19)? Romans 2:18 says that the Bible "is not only a record of God's will; it is also a guideline to determine what course of action is best for us."[30] Further on in Romans, Paul tells us to transform our minds from the current state in order to "test and approve what God's will is—his good, pleasing and perfect will" (12:2).

2. Circumstances: In the days of the Old Testament, the Lord gave His children a very special way to discern His will. Through the use of the Urim and the Thummim, the high priest (leader of the Israelites) was able to inquire about the Lord's will in areas of public concern using either/or, yes/no questions.[31] We no longer have the Urim and Thummim as circumstantial evidence to discern the Lord's will, so it is important to ask certain questions. Is life lining up to make your building campaign happen, or are there closed doors and significant obstacles? (As a word of caution: God often uses circumstances to set the timing, but you can also create seemingly right circumstances under your own strength and then call it "God." Check yourself: is this really God, or are you forcing the issue?) Sometimes the obstacle can involve confrontations and clashes of personality in your leadership team. If so, the importance of a common vision should lead you to question why they are occurring.[32] It might be a sign that it is not God's timing.

3. Leading of the Holy Spirit: What is that still, small voice whispering in your ear? (A word of caution: Sometimes emotion is mistaken as "God." Before jumping to conclusions or mistaking something else for the Spirit's direction, be sure you are at peace and sober minded in seeking God's will. Emotion should not get in the way of hearing his leading.) Just as the Bereans were praised for testing the Scriptures (Acts 17:10-15), you need to test your vision against the Scriptures to make sure that you are truly being Spirit-led. Before Jesus left His disciples on the earth, he claimed that he would send a helper who would teach us all things and remind us of everything Jesus said to us (John 14:26).

4. Godly Council: Seek council from mature believers who have some experience in your current struggle, who know you well, and who will tell you the truth. Listen to them, take notes and pray about all they tell you. (A word of caution: Have you done your due diligence? The work we put in will directly affect the fruit that we reap. Are your eyes wide open? If not, council may not be as useful as it could be.) If David had listened to his council, he may have seen his vision of the building of the temple come to fruition (2 Samuel 7:11-16). Similarly, without the Godly council of a man named Mordecai, the entire nation of Israel may have been stricken from the face of the earth (Esther 9).

5. Prophetic Things: Visions, words of knowledge, prophesies and the like are all examples of this validation. Keep in mind, however, that prophetic things should only be used to confirm your leading from numbers one through four. (A word of caution: Good meaning people often use these things because of a wrong motive, including you!)

Be prepared to abort the take-off if the conditions are not right. If you are doing something against God's will, your project will fail miserably. Remember how Noah's descendants attempted to build without the Lord's leading? What happened to them? I don't know about you, but I do not want to have my entire organization disperse because of undertaking a building campaign that it outside His will!

HOW TO RAISE HORSEPOWER

When the plane is cleared for takeoff, it needs to increase its horsepower in order to take flight. In the same way, an organization's building campaign (once it has been cleared for unobstructed takeoff) needs to pick up steam in order to take flight.

Raising the horsepower of the organization is done by focusing the energy of all who are involved in the process at hand. "All organizations inherently have energy because they are made up of people, and people have energy. But in [successful] organizations, people seem to have more energy, and they certainly use it more productively. While losers waste their energy on negative activities such as internal politics and resisting changes demanded by the marketplace, the winners use theirs positively to overcome problems and meet new challenges."[33]

"Leaders draw others to themselves and their causes, even when the cause is difficult."[34] Leading through this stage of a building campaign can be similar to Joshua and Caleb's attempt to persuade the children of Israel to take the Land that God rightfully gave to them (Num 13:26-33). During this stage, leadership principles may need to coincide with and ask for help from management principles. "Leadership deals with vision—with keeping the mission in sight—and with effectiveness and results. Management deals with establishing structure and systems to get those results. It focuses on efficiency, cost-benefit analyses, logistics, methods, procedures, and policies."[35]

At this point in the building campaign, a good leader will do four things:

> 1. The leader will articulate the vision in such a way that stresses how the values of the organization are being met with the campaign.

> 2. The leader will relinquish certain parts of his or her control by involving people in the decisions on how the campaign helps to achieve the ministry's vision.

> 3. The leader will motivate those involved in the project by providing good coaching, feedback, and role-modeling to help the people grow.

> 4. The leader will recognize and reward the individual successes of the process. This helps to give the people involved a sense of accomplishment as the process continues.[36]

Ultimately, in order to raise enough horsepower on the takeoff, the leader needs to keep the lines of communication open in order to keep the relationships with all constituents strong.[37] Sometimes the communication needs to happen in a one-on-one environment, other times it can be in more massive forms. Sometimes the message needs to be repeated in order to be fully realized. Sometimes the information will be twisted if it is not heard in a direct manner from the leader. Oftentimes communication is negative, but it is always needed. Always remember that communication is a two-way street. "Listen carefully to people and show them you've heard them by responding verbally or taking action."[38]

If you are trying to fly using only your own engine, your plane can only go so far.

If you involve several other engines in the process, it will be easier to get the plane off the ground and into the sky!

ASSESSING YOUR MINISTRY'S POTENTIAL FOR DEVELOPMENT

Step back for a minute and take a good look at your ministry. Have you made sure that your development campaign is within the abilities of the organization? Have you developed a strategic plan for the organization? Does the campaign fit within that plan? Have you created a SWOT analysis for the organization? A SWOT analysis includes the following questions:

• **What are the Strengths of the organization?** What is the organization good at? Is it at the forefront of particular fundraising developments? Does it have access to a donor segment that is not reached by competitors? Does it have a strong database system/great support agencies/high local awareness?

• **What are its Weaknesses?** In what ways do competitors typically outperform the organization? Are there weaknesses in terms of internal support or structures? Are there barriers to future development in some areas?

• **What are the main Opportunities facing the organization over the duration of the plan?** Are there new fundraising techniques to test, new audiences to attract? Are new developments within the organization likely to present extra opportunities for fundraising?

• **What are the major Threats facing the organization?** Is a major competitor likely to launch a new capital appeal? Will economic changes impact certain core donors and leave them with less to give? Are planned changes to legislation likely to curtail fundraising activity?[39]

Take some time to brainstorm about your organization. "Assess your organization by gathering input from your board, staff, and volunteers," and "assess your market by gathering input from your constituents, donors, and community leaders."[40] Answer the following questions as honestly as possible.

1. (STRENGTHS) What three things does our organization do well?

_____

_____

_____

2. (WEAKNESSES) What are three limitations that our organization faces in this challenge?

_____

_____

_____

3. (OPPORTUNITIES) What are three situations upon which our organization can benefit from taking an active approach?

_____

_____

_____

4. (THREATS) What three external things can prevent our organization from reaching its goals?[41]

_____

_____

_____

5. What else does our organization need to accomplish before embarking on this challenge?

_____

_____

_____

"Before you develop a significant, high-impact strategy, you and others on the ministry team should be convinced that a strategy is important and that you need one. Otherwise, the effort will be halfhearted at best."[42]

HOW MUCH MONEY CAN WE RAISE?

Everyone wants to know how much money they can raise. The answer is "it depends." As a rule of thumb you can raise one and a half times to three times your annual undesignated income in a capital campaign over a three year period. Undesignated income is regular budget income, excluding restricted giving, designated giving, project giving, etc.

What does it depend on?

1. The Case
A strong, clear, compelling case will make a huge difference. Many people assume that everyone will understand the case- that everyone will be able to connect the project with the vision. Well, most need help with that. In my experience, most of the time when a fund raising program does not meet its potential it is because the case has not been clearly expressed. This why we have spent so much time this morning on vision and case.

2. Organizational health
Many times, a capital fund raising program will promote unity and health in an organization. It is a time when the vision, mission and values of an organization are presented to everyone. Generally speaking, as people understand what the organization is all about and where it is going they get on board. This builds unity. Occasionally a program like this will expose underlying divisions or hidden agenda. If that happens, there will generally be a negative financial impact.

3. The project itself
Relocation and projects that impact children and youth will more likely result in funding that is 2.5 to 3 times income. It is possible to do more than that but that takes:
- an incredible case
- a very high percentage of participation (normal is 40 to 60%)
- Several major gifts that are each over 10% of the total

Middle range projects include renovations and meeting space (auditoriums, class rooms, dorms, etc.). The hardest projects to fund are:
- Debt reduction – Generally people who joined the organization AFTER the debt was incurred have little ownership of the debt and so tend not to give sacrificially. At the same time, people who have given sacrificially before to the project that still has a debt often feel that they have done their part and look to newcomers to pick up the burden.
- Infrastructure – No one gets excited about giving to drainage ditches, septic systems, parking lots, or even roof repair
- Office space – There is no felt need except amongst the staff

If you have these kinds of projects, join them with ones that are more exciting.

Conclusion

Your plane is almost ready for takeoff. Make sure that all "i's" are dotted and all "t's" are crossed before taxiing out to the runway. By doing so, you will be able to eliminate most of the obstacles that stand between your ministry and its building campaign. Remember, however, that some runway incursions happen at the last moment. It is important to learn how to discern God's will and follow His plan for your entire campaign. Make sure that all of the right people are in full support of the campaign and strapped onto the bus's seats. When you assess the ministry's strengths, weaknesses, opportunities, and threats, be certain you have spent adequate time assessing the ministry's potential for development.

"Blessed is the man who trusts in the Lord, whose confidence is in Him. He will be like a tree planted by the water that sends out its roots by the stream. It does not fear when the heat comes; its leaves are always green. It has no worries in a year of drought and never fails to bear fruit."

—Jeremiah 17:7-8

CHAPTER THREE

THE SCARECROW, THE TIN MAN AND THE COWARDLY LION... SOURCES OF FUNDING

On her journey to see the Wizard of Oz, Dorothy met three characters – the Scarecrow, the Tin Man and the Cowardly Lion. Each one had needs of his own and none was likely to be successful alone. Together they made a formidable force that was able to overcome all obstacles.

With any capital project there are several resources to find funds. Each one has its own needs and agenda. Inviting each source to catch your vision will help to strengthen your resolve and bring organizational success. Realizing that each entity has its own inherent strengths and weaknesses will help you to decide where to put your time and effort. Overall, the five main sources of funds for nonprofit include major gifts, minor (constituent) gifts, grants, corporations, and churches/nonprofit organizations. In most building programs a majority of the funding will come from constituents and major gifts.

Ideally a church will want to get a good portion of the needed capital from each of the five sources, but usually a third will come from major gifts, a third from the constituency, and a third will be brought in by the leadership. If your organization is attempting to raise three times your annual income for this capital project, you will need to make sure that each entity has ample opportunity to buy into the vision!

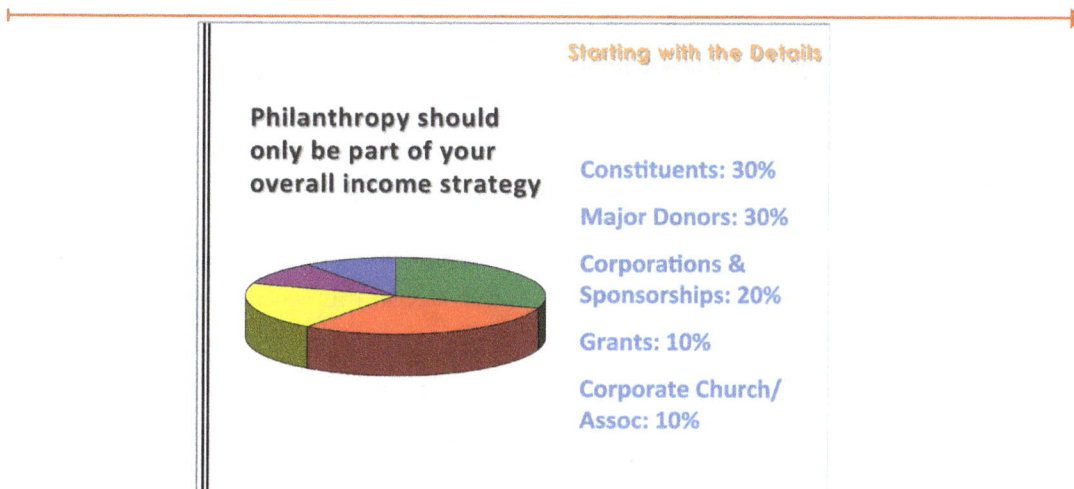

Starting with the Details

Philanthropy should only be part of your overall income strategy

Constituents: 30%

Major Donors: 30%

Corporations & Sponsorships: 20%

Grants: 10%

Corporate Church/ Assoc: 10%

MAJOR GIFTS

Major gifts are defined as those gifts that exceed a set dollar amount. Some organizations set a major gift threshold at $1,000; others set the bar at $25,000. For the sake of the argument, we will set the threshold of the major gifts for capital campaigns at $5,000.

Not everyone has the ability to give a gift of $5,000, but many stakeholders in all organizations can. Potential major donors should be approached early in the campaign to give the campaign a solid and exciting start. Often setting the pace for the project, these early, large commitments are designed to show everyone (including the skeptics) that success is possible. If the desired goal is to raise more than three times the annual income of the organization, this excess will usually come from major donors. It is likely that less than a dozen major gifts (10-12) will raise over one third of the total project goal.

LEADERSHIP COMMITMENTS

If the organization's leadership is not behind this program, why should anyone else support the project? If the leadership does not back it, no one else can be expected to support it. The leadership of the organization can be defined as those who are on the board, on major campaign committees (including the building and fundraising committees), those who have served in strong leadership roles in the past, and those who are key influencers in the church (even if they have no official office). The difference between major gifts and leadership commitments is that major gifts come from those with capacity, and leadership commitments come from those who have willingness (regardless of capacity). Because of their leadership role, these people will have a natural passion for the vision of the church. They also will understand the value of the proposed building in accomplishing that vision before most others will. Leadership commitments should come from about 20% of the constituency and will likely total the second third of the total goal.

CONSTITUENCY

If the old 80/20 rule holds true in all organizations, there are many individuals in your organization who have limited or no involvement in either the leadership or day to day ministry. These individuals may or may not serve in the nonprofit, and they may or may not attend regular events. When posited with a question, however, they will declare that your organization is their organization. To be successful, these individuals will need to be sold on the vision as well as how this project helps to accomplish the vision. Winning these people over will take a lot of effort and an abundance of communication. When most of the stakeholders of the organization have just about had it with all the talk about the building program and the funding campaign, many of these individuals will just be coming aware that something is going on. Never forget that their support is crucial. The goal is to get 50% of this group to make commitments resulting in raising the last third of your goal.

Ideally, your organization does not operate on a budget that is mostly or completely funded by small donations. Do not worry if you currently do, just see it as a goal to diversify your own income. The ideal budgetary breakdown will consist of the following:

a. 30% Major Gifts
b. 30% Minor (Constituency) Gifts
c. 20% Corporations and Sponsorships
d. 10% Grants
e. 10% Churches and other nonprofits

Major Gifts

Major gifts come from people who are already involved in and passionate about your ministry. When these people hear about your need and how it will help the ministry in the long term, they will be generous in their support with gifts over $5,000. Additionally, these people will try to enlist others who can help in a similar manner.

Minor Gifts

Most of the money that organizations receive comes from minor gifts. Starting with your board and staff, ask the people who are passionate about your vision and mission to get involved in the process. Invite everyone who you serve to give to the project. It is likely that organizations will find that those who have benefitted from the ministry will want to return the favor. Encourage all who have benefitted to give back—invite students to give to a school, invite the poor to participate in fundraisers, invite the homeless to showcase their world. The stories of the stakeholders will help to inspire others to give.

Corporations and Sponsorships

Many companies desire to give back to the community. It is not only good public relations for them, but it is also good business. Many will give cash, but some will give services or gifts in kind. Do your homework. Find a contact within the corporation who can tell you who the decision makers are and the history of the corporate donations. Use that information to make an approach to the right people with an appeal that fits the interests and passion of the corporation.

All organizations desire to give back to the community. It is not only good public relations for the organization; it is also good business practice. Corporations are looking to receive the tax deductions that come at the end of the year, but not all will give cash. Some will give services or gifts in kind. After doing a little homework, find a contact within corporations who can give you a list of the decision makers in the community and the corporations' history of donations. Use that information to make an approach to the right people with an appeal that fits the interests and passions of the organizations.

For a little aside: make sure to diversify your income. Many organizations are funded by families—the parents own their own businesses and give on a major donor level. Their kids give on a constituent basis. The businesses contribute to the organizations as well. This is an excellent family to have on board, but this is NOT an example of diversification.

Grants

If corporations and sponsorships are from organizations to which you did not apply, grants are those donations that you did apply to receive. There are many foundations that can help you with bricks and mortar money, but foundations and corporations must be researched to see if they will support you in your endeavors. Doing so has the potential to significantly pay off!

Churches and Other Nonprofits

If churches teach their members to give 10% of their income to the church, should they not also give 10% of their resources to other worthy causes? If you can demonstrate how your project will help a church or other nonprofit fulfill its own mission and vision, you may get some financial support from them. For example, if your project is a community center and the church down the road does not have a gym, they may want to partner with you in exchange for use of that gym for their youth program. Similarly, if your organization is serving the community in a way that other nonprofits cannot, they may want to buy into your way of doing things. Think collaboratively.

DONOR DEVELOPMENT STAGES

Raising funds is a time-consuming and intense process. Unless you are willing to work diligently, the results will be disappointing. The key word in fundraising is "relationships." Pan-handlers are about the only ones who get donations from people they do not know, and they only get pocket change. Every significant donation comes as a result of the development of relationships.

At the beginning of a relationship, a donor will be a prospect. They have never heard your vision, and will not feel urged to give. These people have merely heard your vision, but have never experienced it.

The next stage of giving is usually based on emotion. The giver has heard enough about the organization to tug on their mercy strings. As a result, they feel compelled to give some pocket change to the organization. This gift is merely excess money for them and does not require much effort on the part of the donor. He or she is merely giving money due to an internal guilt that they have and you do not.

The next phase in the giving matrix is to become a constituent. By definition, a constituent is "an essential part."[43] When a donor reaches this level of commitment, they have a definite role in the organization's growth, and their gift will be sacrificial. As Pastor Eric Brown says at Imago Dei church in Seattle, "Giving isn't giving until it interrupts your lifestyle."[44]

The final stage of the giving matrix is to reach the stage of a partner. A partner does not merely say, "How can I?" He or she has a true heart of "How can I?" This is no longer an action but an internal conviction. If any crisis or need befell your ministry, these donors will stand by your side through the thick of it. This is the donor that will see your ministry reach its greatest potential. Consider the following story:

One time I was on the board of a small mission. Needing to take a bathroom break, I left the board meeting. Upon returning, I discovered that I had been elected chairman of the board. As I delved into the inner workings of the mission, I discovered that it was in serious financial difficulty. One of the many unpaid bills was the medical insurance of the missionaries. I needed to raise some funds and I needed to do it fast. Where did I start? I started with Craig and Elda, people that I knew personally and that the capacity to help in significant ways. They were "prospects." They didn't know anything about the mission or the need, but they knew me. As I approached them, explaining the need and asking for their help they quickly became both "donors" and "constituents." At the first meeting I walked out of the meeting with a check that met about 20% of the need. A few hours later, I received a phone call from friends of Craig and Eldas. They were calling to ask if they, too, could give to this need. Craig and Elda became "partners." When they gave money, they invested themselves in the ministry. As partners, they naturally talked about the mission and the need. They motivated others. In this case it happened in a matter of hours. In other cases it will take weeks, months and maybe years but it will pay off.[45]

DONOR DEVELOPMENT STRATEGIES

Once you have identified the various types of potential donors available for your project, you will need to determine a strategy for each group. It may be that you will want to develop a committee for each donor group and task them to develop their own strategy for raising the funds. In general, regardless of the donor group, your strategy will include the following elements:

1. Communication of the long-term vision and mission of the organization

2. Explanation of how this particular project will help the organization fulfill its vision and mission

3. Details on the project—the what, when, where, how and how much

4. Opportunities to give. There are various strategies that you will need to explore in order to find the best one(s) for your donor group:

    a. Matching gifts
    b. Multi-year gifts
    c. One-time gifts
    d. Gifts in kind
    e. Fundraising events
    f. Naming rights

5. Follow-up. All donors want to be appreciated, so an acknowledgement strategy is important.

DONOR DEVELOPMENT COMMITTEES

Once you have determined which donor groups you will approach and what your overall strategy is, you will need to put together a trustworthy committee to do the actual work. Ideally, an executive committee for the campaign will consist of a chairperson, a communications leader, event leaders, and members-at-large.

The chairperson is responsible for the overall management of the committee. He or she will also sit on the steering committee for the entire fundraising project.

The communications leader is responsible to ensure that all communication materials and strategies are in place. He or she must be consistent with the communication strategy of the entire project.

Event leaders are responsible to organization informational meetings, fundraising events, and any other events that the campaign will have.

Members-at-large will be tasked with the direct appeals to potential donors. These members should be chosen according to their expertise and/or relationships with potential donors.

Conclusion

The members of your leadership are crucial to the health and success of your campaign. Do not merely place someone on the team to fill an empty seat. These individuals need to be intrinsically motivated and externally organized. Choose carefully and you will be successful in your quest!

CHAPTER FOUR:
THE RUBY SLIPPERS...
DEVELOPING A COMMUNICATION STRATEGY

Think for a moment about your favorite television commercial. What caught your attention? Did you remember the commercial after the first time you saw it? Believe it or not, advertisers have discovered that individuals must see their advertisement seven times before the consumer remembers the product enough to purchase it. It works thusly:

View #1 – No memory of even seeing the advertisement

View #2 – Can remember something about the ad

View #3 – Irritated at seeing the ad again

View #4 – Remembers the product being advertised

View #5 – If they ever need that product they will choose the advertised brand

View #6 – Someday I want one of those

View #7 – I have to have one

The key to communication is redundancy. Repetition usually equates importance. The problem with communication is this: at the same time that the decision makers begin to question the expenses and efforts put into all the communication, those who need to know are just discovering the material.

Dorothy's ruby slippers were a symbol. They represented who she was and what she was doing. They communicated for her. In the same way, you will need a communication strategy.

DEVELOP A CAMPAIGN SLOGAN AND LOGO

A catchy phrase or slogan with a visual logo and a strategically-chosen verse will brand your program and make it much easier for potential donors to identify the campaign and remember your need. Remember back to the parking lot campaign from Chapter 2. The slogan that church chose was "Forward by Faith: That My House Might be Full." The slogan captured the idea that the project was for the future and that it should produce the results of increased attendance. It had the added benefit of referencing scripture.

1. Considering your audience, what do you want to say to get people's attention?

_____
_____
_____
_____
_____
_____

2. How do you want to say it?

_____
_____
_____
_____
_____
_____

3. What Scripture verses come to mind when you consider your ministry's future?

_____
_____
_____
_____
_____
_____

4. If you had to sum up your quest in one sentence, what would you say?

_____
_____
_____

5. Will your slogan be transferrable to all the generations/cultures in your audience? Why/why not?

_____
_____
_____
_____
_____

WRITE DOWN THE CASE IN A PAGE

This was referenced previously, but the case needs to be written clearly, concisely, and completely. Additionally, this case statement needs to be approved by all of the board members and everyone else that is involved in the process. If campaigns begin on the wrong foot, most often it is due to disgruntled members of the leadership who were not involved in the final decision of the case.

BEGIN TO LEAK THE NEWS

The best way to create some initial buzz in the organization is to send out a newsletter or other regular communication to the stakeholders that merely explains the fact that something is coming soon. This form of communication will get people talking and asking questions. The most difficult part is not spilling the beans before the time is right, however. Remember: Loose lips sink ships.

DEVELOP A BROCHURE

In today's visual society, information needs to be easily disseminated in a clear, concise manner. The best way to do so is to develop a visually-appealing brochure or coffee table piece. Better yet, consider producing a visual presentation on CD-ROM or DVD. Whatever you decide to develop, make sure that it addresses the vision, mission, case, and building project. Include specific details such as cost, building timeline, program timeline, etc.

MORE SPECIFIC NEWSLETTERS

After creating the coffee table piece, begin to prepare 2-3 specific, detailed newsletters. These will begin to detail the costs, fundraising goals, fundraising team, and other things. Make sure to include stories from individuals that will encourage the readers to sacrifice where they feel led. These newsletters would be an excellent place to develop and deliver devotionals to the constituents. The newsletters can also serve as an informational piece describing the future informational meetings, commitment events, etc.

SEND OUT REMINDER CARDS

Most people have a difficult time remembering what they had for breakfast; let alone what is going on in your building campaign. Take the time to prepare and send out reminder postcards to let people know about up and coming events. Though this will cost you a little bit more in postage, it will be read by more people than an email.

CREATE PRAYER REMINDERS

If you truly believe in the power of prayer, why not use it? The constituents for your organization need to be reminded to pray for your campaign and the circumstances surrounding the campaign. Why not create a prayer calendar to include in the newsletters? Make sure to carve out specific prayer requests for certain dates. If you cannot think of good requests for specific days, then consider putting all of the requests down on a card that can be used as a bookmark. However you can, make sure to remind the people with whom you come into contact to pray for the campaign as often as they think about it.

CREATE COMMITMENT CARDS

Commitment cards are your key to success and need to be well-written. It doesn't need to be fancy, but it does need to be something that catches people's attention. You want people to pick up the card, read it, and respond to it positively. After creating a rough draft, hand it out to personal friends to see what they would want to see changed to help tug on their heart strings.

THE COMMUNICATION PROCESS

Have you ever stopped to think about the meaning behind the words, "Rome was not built in a day." Okay, so how many days did it take? What steps were involved in the building of the greatest city in the ancient world?

Know that in your building campaign, you will not get from Point A (where you are) to Point B (where you want to "B"—pun intended) overnight. It will take months of careful planning, plotting, prodding and producing to get to that final destination. Enjoy the ride, for it could be a roller-coaster experience!

In order to produce a solid product at the end of your building campaign, you need to nail down a few details. Make sure that you set an achievable timeframe. Envision the possible potholes along the way and plan how to avoid falling into them. Take the time to develop a strategy for how you will build your Rome. Enlist the help of several trustworthy friends in order to help keep your vision clear and honest. This chapter will help you to prepare for the process ahead. Setting goals is one of the most important things that you can do for your building campaign. If you have not yet done this, take a moment to pray for God to guide you in the goal-setting process. After all, if He gave you the vision, He will help you to carry it on to completion. "For I am confident of this very thing, that He who began a good work in you will perfect it until the day of Christ Jesus" (Phil 1:6, NASB).

SETTING AN ACHIEVABLE TIMEFRAME

Have you ever seen an Amish barn raising? Whether you have or not, listen to the following account of an actual event:

> I was invited to a barn raising near Wooster, Ohio. A tornado had leveled four barns and acres of prime Amish timber. In just three weeks the downed trees were sawn into girders, posts, and beams and the four barns rebuilt and filled with livestock donated by neighbors to replace those killed by the storm. Three weeks. Nor were the barns the usual modern, one-story metal boxes hung on poles. They were huge buildings, three and four stories high, post-and-beam framed, and held together with hand-hewn mortises and tenons. I watched the raising of the last barn in open-mouthed awe. Some 400 Amish men and boys, acting and reacting like a hive of bees in absolute harmony of cooperation, started at sunrise with only a foundation and floor and by noon, by noon, had the huge edifice far enough along that you could put hay in it.

> A contractor who was watching said it would have taken him and a beefed-up crew all summer to build the barn if, indeed, he could find anyone skilled enough at mortising to do it. He estimated the cost at $100,000. I asked the Amish farmer how much cash he would have in the barn. "About $30,000," he said. Some of that would be paid out by the Amish church's own insurance arrangements. "We give each other our labor," he explained. "We look forward to raisings. There are so many helping, no one has to work too hard. We get in a good visit."[47]

Now let me test your understanding with this question: How long did it take the Amish men to build that barn from scratch? Twenty-four hours? Twelve hours? Six hours? Less time than that? No, wrong, it was much longer than that! It took them over three weeks! I can hear the questions now—"What?!? It says they started at dawn and finished at noon. That is less than one day!"

Read the third sentence again, and note how much time it takes to help raise a barn in a day!

So, how long should it take for your building campaign? What is an "achievable timeframe" for this project? All of these questions depend on several residual factors. For example, how much are you, the leader, willing to work? How many people will be working on the campaign? Where is the project located? What does the community think of the project? How long does each step take?

HOW MUCH
ARE YOU WILLING TO WORK?

Some leaders are 8-5 leaders. They show up at the office a few minutes before it opens at 8:00 and leave a few minutes after the doors close at 5:00. Other leaders give 12 hours per day to the business. Still others hold no particular "office hours." These people are answering phones and/or email messages at all hours of the day and night.

Has it ever dawned on you that an individual working merely 8 hours per day may get just as much done as another individual working 18 hours per day? "Work smarter, not harder" is the management cliché from the 1990s, but it is one that is not practiced enough.

Have you taken the time to prioritize your schedule? Consider this: some things need to get done now, some need to get done later. Some things would be nice to get done now, some would be nice to get done later. Stephen Covey says that there are four quadrants of time management that would help to prioritize your life, if you follow them. "Quadrant I is both urgent and important. It deals with significant results that require immediate attention. We usually call the activities in Quadrant I 'crises' or 'problems.'…[this quadrant] consumes many people. They are crisis managers, problem-minded people, deadline-driven producers."[48] Quadrant II encompasses things that are important but not urgent. These things may include planning, relationship-building, and recreation time. They are important to maintaining a balanced and healthy lifestyle, but it's not necessary to accomplish them immediately. Quadrant III includes urgent, unimportant tasks such as interruptions, phone calls, emails, and other pressing matters. Quadrant IV includes unimportant, non-urgent tasks that are a trivial pursuit.[49]

Personal time-management skills need to be practiced during your building campaign or you will suffer burn-out! If time management is not one of your strengths, consider employing the help of a trusted friend or mentor to keep you accountable to your tasks. If you are not sure what your strengths are, consider purchasing the book by Marcus Buckingham and Donald O. Clifton, *Now, Discover Your Strengths*[50] or another book that will help you evaluate your gifts. Setting personal boundaries during this time in your ministry's life is one of the first steps to success. Make sure to write down your boundaries and timelines, read them once per week, and stick to them. Use the following as a guide to help you get through the challenging building campaign in one piece:

1. I will relax every week by_____

2. I will maintain time-management accountability with _____

3. I will not answer phone calls or emails between the hours of _____

4. I will date my spouse on this day of the week _____

5. I will tell my children that I love them _____times per day.

"Getting people to do what's best—for customers, for the business, even for themselves—is often a struggle because it means getting people to understand and want to do what's best, and that requires integrity, the willingness to empower others, courage, tenacity, and great teaching skills."[51] Just because you are able to get something done yourself does not mean that you should. Delegate the authority to do certain things to other people within or outside the organization. Good delegation skills can take a load off any leader!

HOW MANY PEOPLE ARE WORKING?

Listen carefully: You are NOT Superman. Superman was a creation of Jerry Siegel and Joe Shuster in the 1930s.[52] You are a human being with certain limitations. The skills that you lack, however, may be the strengths of other members of your team!

How well do you know the people who are working with you on this campaign? Where do you complement each other? What strengths do others have that you do not? Consider the following scenario:

> Most organizations are a puzzle put together in a darkened room. Each piece is clumsily squeezed into place and then the edges are ground down so that they feel well positioned. But pull up the shades, let a little light into the room, and we can see the truth. Eight out of ten pieces are in the wrong place.

> Eight out of ten employees feel they are miscast. Eight out of ten employees never have the chance to reveal the best of themselves. They suffer for it, their organization suffers, and their customers suffer. Their health, their friends, and their family suffer.[53]

Whether or not you pay people to help you with the project, every person who assists you in the building campaign should be given the proper tools and the opportunity to use their gifts. When volunteers and staff are used in areas outside their strengths, not only is their energy sapped, but their willingness to continue helping depletes. There's a simple solution. Most people "can learn to modify their behavior to accomplish goals or perform more effectively [and are] most likely to do so if you've given them the tools to do the job."[54]

Many hands may make light work, but those hands need to be skilled in the areas in which they are involved. During the 2006 fiscal year, 26,196 homes were either built or rehabilitated by Habitat for Humanity.[55] In the Gulf Coast states alone, 32,000 volunteers offered to help with the rebuilding efforts following Hurricanes Rita and Katrina.[56] How many people you have working on a capital campaign will have a huge impact on how long the campaign takes.

WHERE IS THE PROJECT LOCATED?

If your project is located in Medora, North Dakota (Zip Code: 58645), the project's duration from conception to completion will be much longer than if your project is located in Lewisville, Texas (Zip Code: 75067). Why is this? Medora is located in the Badlands of Southwest North Dakota, 33 miles from the nearest "big city" of Dickinson (population < 20,000). Lewisville is centrally located in the Northern suburbs of the Dallas-Fort Worth Metroplex (population around 5,000,000). "Location, Location, Location" is an important factor in how long the project will take.

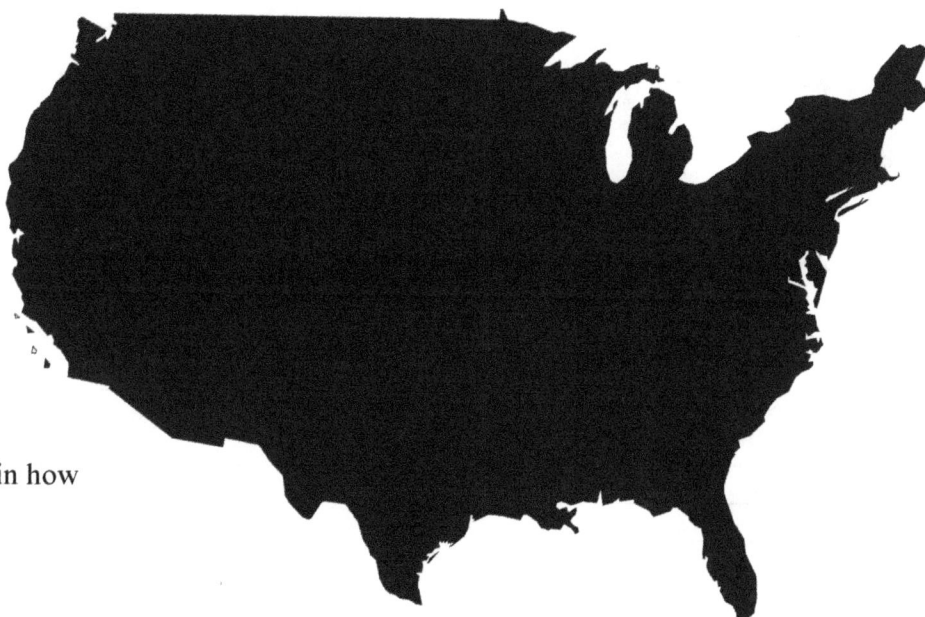

WHAT IS THE COMMUNITY'S INVOLVEMENT?

Don't forget what David Steward said about how people will support what they help to create. Make sure to include as many people as possible in each stage of the campaign and ensure that the entire community realizes how the campaign will benefit the community at large.[57] "'New blood' is an important concept to non-profit organizations. The down side of constantly looking for new blood is that the task never ends."[58] The upside to the community's involvement is that they will catch your vision and desire to see you succeed in what you are doing. How involved the community is in the building campaign is an important step to consider in how long the project will last.

How Long Does Each Step Take?

Answer this question: Right now, what does your ministry look like?

_____
_____
_____
_____
_____

In 12 months (1 year), what do you want it to look like?

_____
_____
_____
_____
_____

Now comes the difficult part: How do you get from Point A to Point B? Will your building campaign be done in that one year? Remember that how long the campaign takes depends on many factors (personal work ethic, volunteer or other involvement, location, and outside involvement). Set a goal for the completion of the campaign. "In 12/ 18/ 24/ 30/ 36 months (circle one), the campaign will be completed." The finished target needs to be established before the arrows can be launched. Next, create some solid action steps (no more than 7 total) that will take you from where you are to where you want to be. Place a solid, dated deadline on each one of those steps. Underneath each step, write down between one and three different strategies that you will use to accomplish that step toward the goal.[59] By putting the end product on paper, creating action steps to get there, and brainstorming different strategies to complete each step, you will increase the overall likelihood of taking the ministry from where it is to where you want it to be!

TO-DO LIST:

1.

2.

3.

PLANNING FOR AND AVOIDING PITFALLS

"Be self-controlled and alert. Your enemy the devil prowls around like a roaring lion looking for someone to devour. Resist him, standing firm in the faith, because you know that your brothers throughout the world are undergoing the same kind of sufferings" (1 Pet 5:8-9). If you have not already figured it out, your campaign will face several attacks. Planning for those attacks and avoiding certain ones will do nothing but help your campaign.

Do you remember the SWOT analysis that you completed in the previous chapter? The Weaknesses and Threats from that analysis are the areas that will most likely come back to haunt you.

Consider the story of Samson and Delilah in the Old Testament book of Judges. Samson had one strong weakness—women—and one strong threat—having a haircut. So what did Samson do? First of all, Samson went into the city of Gaza, found a prostitute, and spent the night with her (Jud 16:1). After this, he fell in love with a woman who was constantly trying to pry secrets from him (v. 4-5). Finally, he divulged the secret of his strength to this deceiver and lost his God-given abilities (v. 17-21).

It is easy to look upon Samson's mistakes and poke fun at the Lord's judge, but he should stand out as a solid example of how to plan for and avoid pitfalls. Consider how Samson knew before hand that he had a weakness for women (Chapter 14). He also knew (before he was born) that he was set apart to do great things for God (Chapter 13).

Look back at your Weaknesses and Threats. Now that they are fresh in your memory, take five minutes on each weakness and five minutes on each threat and think about ways that those two areas could cause your organization's (or your personal) downfall.

1. For each one of your weaknesses, write at least two ways that your organization could succumb to that pitfall.

_____
_____
_____
_____
_____
_____

2. For each one of your threats, write at least two ways that your organization could succumb to that pitfall.

_____
_____
_____
_____
_____
_____

Make sure to keep your SWOT analysis handy at all times and constantly refer back to it. Keeping those weaknesses and threats at the forefront of your thought will help you to remember to avoid those pitfalls. Another good idea is to become friends with a good lawyer. Better yet, find yourself a good trusted counselor. "Trusted counselors are people who know you and your business. They are strategists—people who can factor legal risk into a business decision…[They] see themselves as officers of the court whose professional responsibility includes preventing their clients from committing crimes…It takes time and effort to develop relationships with trusted legal counselors, and sometimes you will not like what they tell you. But they are valuable advisers who will protect you from a world of trouble."[60]

DEVELOPING A STRATEGIC CAMPAIGN

Hopefully by now you have created a mission and vision for your ministry, performed a SWOT analysis, and created the framework for your campaign. Now it is time to make sure that your building campaign has a strategy. If you enjoy playing chess, checkers, backgammon, or other strategy games (as opposed to games of complete chance), you just may find this area exciting!

Have you ever heard the mantra, "it is easier to see ahead if you stand on the shoulders of those before you?" One of the greatest parts about this portion of your campaign is that you can utilize the resources of other people who have been where you are. No matter if you are a church, an orphanage, a camp, an office, or a service-oriented non-profit organization, there has been an organization just like you who has been through this process in the past. Find those organizations, call up their leadership, and ask questions. Becoming good friends with them during this process is a great idea! Think about it this way: Why are you reading this book? Are you not trying to get some inside knowledge on the entire process? Of course you are, and you should be applauded for your efforts!

As you embark on this process, you may find yourself in a mode of procrastination. After all, strategizing is a workout for your mind, and it can be no simple task! Following are ten steps or strategies to help you as you develop your strategic campaign:[61]

1. **Focus on your top five priorities.**

    Looking at the mountain in front of you can be intimidating, but taking the first small steps will help you to realize that the process has begun. Find out what the five most important issues of your campaign are and nail down a plan to accomplish them in the near future. Set a time frame on when to have each task accomplished and stick to it!

2. **Something is always better than nothing.**

    It would be great if you could snap your fingers and be completely finished with the campaign, but that will not happen. If you are chosen to have your organization featured on *Extreme Makeover: Home Edition* and have the project completed in five days by professionals, congratulations. If you are like most of the rest of the world, you just need to get started.

3. **Begin the process as soon as possible.**

    All missions are works in progress. Did you know that Mark Twain had Tom Sawyer in his mind for over five years? "He had worked and reworked [the novel] until he could no longer judge its aesthetic worth."[62] The problem is that it takes longer to accomplish something if it is never started!

4. **Move one stone at a time.**

    Herod the Great was an exceptional builder around the time that Jesus Christ came to earth. One of his greatest building accomplishments was his palace and burial grounds called the Herodium. Believe it or not, the mountain upon which the Herodium was build is an artificial mountain. That's right, Herod literally moved a mountain![63] Looking at the project today, you might think that the task was impossible. Seeing the completed project is mind-boggling, but remember that the entire project was completed one stone at a time.

5. **Consider writing your strategy in one day.**

    Some people excel when they take a large chunk of continuous time to accomplish a certain task. Others need small blocks of time spaced out to accomplish the same task. Only you know yourself. Are you the kind of person who needs to barricade yourself in a room with no phone, television, or other distractions and write until the strategy is complete; or are you the kind of person who can devote 5-10 minutes per day on the task? Either way, make sure that you take breaks to refresh your mind and have some fun in the process.

6. **Leave.**
   If your campaign is the talk of the town, you may not be able to get uninterrupted time to work on your strategy in town. Take a day or a couple of days to get away from the city to get your strategy completed.

7. **Have someone else do it.**
   This can be very dangerous, so listen closely. If you cannot get the project completed by yourself, have others help you write certain portions of the strategy. Ensure that those people are trustworthy and knowledgeable about your mission and vision. If you chose to seek help in this way, try to set up meeting times with that person(s) to discuss the overall project and to make sure that you are on the same wavelength.

8. **Do not try to be perfect.**
   During this phase, your goal should be to get something written down in the amount of time that you have set aside. Don't strive for perfect English/Spanish/grammar. Just strive to get something in writing. Proofreading your strategy can be done by somebody (anybody) else. After all, you are more apt to miss your own grammatical errors than you are the errors of others.

9. **Make it a team effort.**
   This campaign is (hopefully) not yours alone. You may have dozens of other people who are just waiting for you to ask for their help. No man or woman is an island, and two heads are always better than one. Get everyone involved in the process, and they will catch the vision of the project. When everyone catches the vision, you can ride the wave to the finish line.

10. **Just do it.**
    "Sometimes getting your plan done just requires a little push. So here is your push!"[64] In the words of Larry the Cable Guy, "Git-R-Done!"[65]

THE IMPORTANCE OF HONESTY AND CLEAR VISION

O Lord my God, I take refuge in you; save and deliver me from all who pursue me, or they will tear me like a lion and rip me to pieces with no one to rescue me. O Lord my God, if I have done this and there is guilt on my hands—if I have done evil to him who is at peace with me or without case have robbed my foe—then let my enemy pursue and overtake me; let him trample my life to the ground and make me sleep in the dust.

Selah.

Arise, O Lord, in your anger; rise up against the rage of my enemies. Awake, my God; decree justice. Let the assembled peoples gather around you. Rule over them from on high; let the Lord judge the peoples. Judge me, O Lord, according to my righteousness, according to my integrity, O Most High. O righteous God, who searches minds and hearts, bring to an end the violence of the wicked and make the righteous secure.

—Psalm 7

Without honesty, a man is not worth much. "Lack of integrity can undermine almost any other effort to create high trust accounts. People can seek to understand, remember the little things, keep their promises, clarify and fulfill expectations, and still fail to build reserves of trust if they are inwardly duplicitous."[67] If you take nothing away from this chapter, take this statement: Be honest with yourself. In your heart, you know whether or not you can accomplish the goals you set. In your heart, you know whether or not your ministry has a clear vision. In your heart, you know whether your mission is to serve God or serve yourself. In your heart, you know whether you desire personal gain or to see God's Kingdom advanced. Only you and God can truly know your heart. David was able to pray, "Search me, O God, and know my heart; test me and know my anxious thoughts. See if there is any offensive way in me, and lead me in the way everlasting" (*Psalm 139:23-24*). Are you able to honestly pray the same prayers?

Conclusion

Goal-setting is one of the most difficult parts of a building campaign. It involves detailed, mind-bending work that is necessary to help the organization realize their dreams and build strong foundations for the future. This detail-oriented step is extremely important in the building campaign. When setting the goals, make sure to have an achievable timeframe, lookout for the potential pitfalls along the way, develop a strategic game plan, and enlist the help of some trustworthy friends.

"...[We] are always confident and know that as long as we are at home in the body we are away from the Lord. We live by faith, not by sight. We are confident, I say, and would prefer to be away from the body and at home with the Lord. So we make it our goal to please Him, whether we are at home in the body or away from it."

—2 Corinthians 5:6-9

CHAPTER FIVE:
THE YELLOW BRICK ROAD...

THE NEXT STEPS

What are some of the most superhuman feats that man can accomplish while on earth? Climb Mount Everest? Swim the English Channel? Win the Boston Marathon? No matter what accomplishment you can think about, remember that each person who accomplishes those feats began somewhere.

Welcome to "somewhere." You are at a place where you are beginning the climb, the swim, the race. This workbook will not help you to climb the mountain, swim the stream, or run the race. Those who have climbed, swum, and run began at the beginning: the preparation.

Where you are is where you need to be right now in your building campaign. This workbook is laying down a few of the steps that you will need to consider in the climb. It has told you a little bit about what it will take to get from the base camp to the summit.

This final chapter will help you to begin to rise to a higher level by taking some short-term action steps.

RISING TO A HIGHER LEVEL

When John Hunt began to recall the account of Sir Edmund Hillary and Sherpa Tenzing Norgay's first ascent of Mount Everest in 1953, he said:

> ...[The] ascent of Everest was not the work of one day, nor even of those few anxious, unforgettable weeks in which we prepared and climbed last spring. It [was] a sustained and tenacious endeavor by many, over a long period of time. To unfold the whole of this long-drawn-out drama within the compass of this book would either make it so broad a survey as to be dull reading, or else fail to do justice to some of those who took part. Moreover, these earlier feats have already been competently told of in detail and summarized by others. So I will do no more than sketch the past in barest outline.

> It is now well over thirty years since an expedition was first sent to explore the mountain with the serious intention of making a subsequent attempt to climb it. Since that date, 1921, no less than eleven major expeditions have followed one another, eight of them with the definite mission to get to the top. In the course of three of these expeditions, at least four British climbers, in 1924 and 1933, and last year a Sherpa and a Swiss together, arrived within about 1,000 feet of the peak, only to be forced back at the limit of endurance or by climatic or snow conditions. In addition, there have been several minor expeditions to Everest by small parties, or even by individuals. It is also worth remembering that a number of lives have been lost in attempts to reach the summit.[67]

Your ministry has the potential to reach the summit, but you also have the potential to come up short or die along the way. Short term action steps are needed to make sure that your desire to get to the top becomes a reality!

SHORT TERM ACTION STEPS

In case you haven't quite figured it out, the building campaign is an endurance run. The length of the course is a relative question. Just like any other race, you need to get ready, get set, and then go!

Get Ready

Are you ready for this? No, I mean are *you* personally ready for this? You need to be internally and externally ready for the things that are to come. Your internal preparation is between you and God. What are you doing to prepare yourself for this race? Have you distanced yourself from God during this initial stage or have you drawn closer to Him? Listen to some fatherly advice from the Proverbs (3:1-6):

> "My son, do not forget my teaching, but keep my commands in your heart, for they will prolong your life many years and bring you prosperity. Let love and faithfulness never leave you; bind them around your neck, write them on the tablet of your heart. Then you will win favor and a good name in the sight of God and man. Trust in the Lord with all your heart and lean not on your own understanding; in all your ways acknowledge him, and he will make your paths straight."

"Trust must precede any honest request of God."[68] Have you trusted and asked God to help you in this stage of your ministry? If not, please take some time to do that before reading any further.

Now that you are internally ready for this race, you must figure out whether you are externally ready for this race. Who do you have with you on this bus?[69] Have you asked other people to evaluate yourself and your ministry before committing to this race? Ask trusted individuals in your life to do a SWOT analysis on this campaign as it pertains to you. In other words, ask your friends to point out where they think your strengths and weaknesses lie, and what they believe will be your greatest opportunities and threats.

Carve out some time to spend with each of the at least three different people who performed a SWOT analysis on you and ask them to be brutally honest. Following these analyses, make sure to prayerfully and thoughtfully consider everything that they noted. Did they mention anything that you need to work on before you begin this campaign? If so, consider the costs of a decision to either take some time to work on those areas or to forge ahead with the plans for the campaign.

Get Set

Is your corporation, community, and constituency ready for this campaign both internally and externally? First and foremost, consider whether your organization is internally ready for such a long, grueling race. Does this campaign fit within your organization's vision, mission, and goals? Are you trying to glorify God with the campaign, or are you trying to make a name for yourself and your ministry?

Don't forget to check the level of oil in your organization. How does the staff feel about the upcoming campaign? Has there been an open forum for all of the internal people of ministry to speak freely regarding the upcoming race? If not, have one! If there has been, have you taken all of their comments to heart? Do you need to change your plans at all to make sure that everyone is on the same page? Do you need to spend some more time educating your helpers to make sure that they know how this campaign will help the organization to fulfill its vision and mission?

On the outside, are the community and the people you serve supportive of this campaign? If they are not, is there a reason for their hesitancy? Make sure to check their level of oil to understand why they are ready or why they are hesitating in their support for your campaign. Gauging the readiness of the internal and external members of your ministry is an important step in getting set for the campaign.

Determine which committees you want to enlist to help in the process and the leadership roles inherent in each committee. Develop a timeline that includes target dates for completion from each donor group. Get your campaign materials prepared and print several copies to be used over and over again (print it on good quality paper and consider laminating it!).

Once you have made sure that you personally are internally and externally prepared; and once you have ensured the internal and external preparation of your ministry, it is time to get rolling. This can be done in five simple steps:

1. Pray to begin the process (and continually throughout!) Remember who it is that gives you the resources to do what you are doing. If God is not involved in the process from the start, your campaign will fail.

2. Order the process to begin. Make the first call to the contractor or fundraiser or foreman to let them know that the process is a go.

3. Regularly check on the process's progress. Keep an eye on the campaign's progress. Constantly make sure that the campaign is inline with the organization's mission, vision, and goals.

4. Seek help when you need it. You do not know everything about the process, nor should you. If you need an expert's advice in any area, get it! Remember that there are organizations like ours who exist to help your organization build your foundation and realize your dreams.

5. Let the professionals do their jobs. It may be difficult to refrain from a micromanaging mindset, but you must do so. Professionals have years of experience in their areas, and you hired them to do their jobs. Make sure to use them as much as possible to get your money's worth, but realize that they may tell you things that you do not want to hear. If you want a second opinion in an area, seek it out. Otherwise, make sure to follow the advice of the professionals.

CHECKLIST

1. Prayer

2. Personal Preparation:

- This program will not help you spiritually, it will likely test your spiritual heath. So do not go into this if you are close to a spiritual burnout.

- The same is true emotionally and physically.

- Financially: If you as a leader can not sacrificially and proportionately give significant financial support perhaps this is not the time. You must be able to lead financially for this to be successful. This does not mean that you have to make the largest gift but you have to lead in terms of sacrifice.

3. Organizational Preparation

- Vision, Mission, Values and Goals – set the foundation.

- Have your building plan ready with at least some of the costs known. Few will give if you say "we plan to build something but it will be determined by how much we raise."

- Have the Case developed.

- Make sure your leadership is on board.

    - Make sure that your staff is on board. They need to be both in the loop and supportive (including financially). Without their support you will be trouble.

    - The Board must be on board. They should be willing to make their commitments early on, and these commitments need to add up to a significant amount of money.

    - Talk to your major supporters – those who regularly support the work year in and year out. You can not afford to have them stop giving to the regular budget.

4. Program Preparation:

- Detailed timelines.

Overall timeline and plan:
- When do you want to start building work? This becomes the date from which you work backwards.

- Your goal should be to have commitments in place no more than 18 months before you plan to build (any longer and people will be frustrated in waiting to see something happen and stop giving).

- You will need 3 to 6 months of intensive fund raising time.

- You will need 3-6 months prior to the intensive fund raising time to get the Case developed, enlist leaders and get the communication pieces in place.

Timeline for each donor group:
- Leadership Gifts: This is generally the first place to start. Until it is demonstrated that your leadership (Staff and Board) are committed to the project, no one needs to take you seriously.

- Major Gifts: Next develop the time frame for soliciting Major Gifts. This will bring encouragement to the Consitituency and to outside donors.

- When you have these timelines done, you will be able to determine what the timeline looks like for the Communication Strategy.

- Communication Strategy:
  - Determine what pieces you will use (web presence, brochure, newsletters, DVD, reminders, prayer pieces, etc) and when they will be ready and distributed.

  - Leadership – Determine what positions are needed, and write a job description for each one along with timelines and deadlines.

- Clear the organizational calendar – There must be a focus on the fund raising efforts. You cannot simply add this program on top of your regular activities. It is a mistake to have a golf tournament to raise funds for the general budget while you are seeking new funds for your building program. At the same time, you can not stop your regular programs and ministries. The key here is to make sure that the fundraising efforts are not lost in the midst of other announcements, programs and efforts. Nor should there be competition for financial gifts (with the exception of your regular budget needs).

Conclusion

You are now ready to run your race, climb your mountain, and swim your channel. You have solidified your organization's mission and vision. You have made sure that the level of oil in your organization is correct and ready for the process. You have made sure that the runway is clear of any incursions that could be deadly to your process. You have created some solid goals to help you get from Point A to Point B. Now you just need to take those first steps!

Enjoy the process, and remember that we are here if you need us!

"May the Lord answer you when you are in distress; may the name of the God of Jacob protect you. May He send you help from the sanctuary and grant you support from Zion. May He remember all your sacrifices and accept your burnt offerings. Selah. May He give you the desire of your heart and make all your plans succeed. We will shout for joy when you are victorious and will lift up our banners in the name of our God. May the Lord grant all your requests."

—*Psalm 20:1-5*

ENDNOTES

1 Andy Stanley, Visioneering: God's Blueprint for Developing and Maintaining Personal Vision (Colorado Springs: Multnomah Publishers, Inc., 2001).

2 H. Darrell Young and Joseph P. Hester, Leadership under Construction: Creating Paths toward Transformation (Oxford: ScarecrowEducation, 2004).

3 Lorin Woolfe, The Bible on Leadership: From Moses to Matthew: Management Lessons for Contemporary Leaders (New York: AMACOM, 2002).

4 Craig Hickman and Michael A. Silva, Creating Excellence (New York: New American Library, 1984).

5 Burt Nanus, Visionary Leadership (San Francisco: Jossey-Bass Inc., 1992).

6 Peter M. Senge, "Leadership in Living Organizations," in Leading Beyond the Walls, ed. Frances Hesselbein, Marshall Goldsmith, and Iain Somerville (San Francisco: Jossey-Bass Inc., 1999).

7 Noel M. Tichy and Mary Anne Devanna, The Transformational Leader: The Key to Global Competitiveness (New York: John Wiley & Sons, Inc., 1990).

8 James C. Hunter, The World's Most Powerful Leadership Principle: How to Become a Servant Leader (New York: Crown Business, 2004).

9 Richard L. Moreland and Linda Argote, "Transactive Memory in Dynamic Organizations," in Leading and Managing People in the Dynamic Organization, ed. Randall S. Peterson and Elizabeth A. Mannix (Mahwah, NJ: Lawrence Erlbaum Associates, 2003).

10 Anita Hall, Leverne Barrett, and Cheryl Burkhart-Kriesel, "Developing a Vision for the Community or Organization," NebGuide (2005).

11 Tichy and Devanna.

12 John P. Kotter, Leading Change (Boston: Harvard Business School Press, 1996).

13 Ann McGee-Cooper and Duane Trammell, "From Hero-as-Leader to Servant-as-Leader," in Focus on Leadership: Servant-Leadership for the 21st Century, ed. Larry C. Spears and Michele Lawrence (New York: John Wiley & Sons, Inc., 2002).

14 Ibid.

15 Young and Hester.

16 Nanus.

17 David Campbell, "Nine Keys to Good Leadership," in The Ccl Guide to Leadership in Action: How Managers and Organizations Can Improve the Practice of Leadership, ed. Martin Wilcox and Stephen Rush (San Francisco: Jossey-Bass Inc., 2004).

18 Ken Blanchard, "Turning Vision into Reality: Leadership Is Not Something You Do to People; It's Somethinmg You Do with Them," Christianity Today, April 17 2006.

19 Kotter, Andy Stanley, "Vision Leaks: How Do You Keep the Church's Passion for Ministry from Deflating?," Leadership Journal 25, no. 1 (2004).

20 Hall, Barrett, and Burkhart-Kriesel.

21 Nanus.

22 Hall, Barrett, and Burkhart-Kriesel.

23 Nanus.

24 Ibid.

25 These validations will be explained further in the coming chapters.

26 Stephen C. Harper, The Forward-Focused Organization: Visionary Thinking and Breakthrough Leadership to Create Your Company's Future (New York: AMACOM, 2001).

27 Nanus.

28 Kathleen O'Brien, The Runway Incursion Problem (Washington, DC: Federal Aviation Administration, 2005), 1.

29 James L. Garlow, The 21 Irrefutable Laws of Leadership Tested by Time: Those Who Followed Them and Those Who Didn't (Nashville: Thomas Nelson Publishers, 2002), 14.

30 Bruce B. Barton, David R. Veerman, and Neil Wilson, Romans, ed. Grant Osborne, Life Application Bible Commentary (Wheaton, IL: Tyndale House Publishers, Inc., 1992), 54.

31 David J. Zucker, The Torah: An Introduction for Christians and Jews (New York: Paulist Press, 2005), 108.

32 Regina E. Herzlinger, "Culture Is the Key," in Leading Beyond the Walls, ed. Frances Hesselbein, Marshall Goldsmith, and Iain Somerville (San Francisco: Jossey-Bass, Inc., 1999).

33 Noel M. Tichy and Eli Cohen, The Leadership Engine: How Winning Companies Build Leaders at Every Level (New York: HarperCollins Publishers, Inc., 1997, 2002), 162.

34 Garlow, 27.

35 Stephen R. Covey, Principle-Centered Leadership (New York: Fireside, 1990, 1991), 246.

36 Adapted from John P. Kotter, "What Leaders Really Do," in Harvard Business Review on Leadershsip (Boston: Harvard Business School Press, 1998), 48.

37 Scott Campbell and Ellen Samiec, 5-D Leadership: Key Dimensions for Leading in the Real World (Mountain View, CA: Davies-Black Publishing, 2005), 187.

38 Lorin Woolfe, Leadership Secrets from the Bible: From Moses to Matthew--Management Lessons for Contemporary Leaders (New York: Barnes & Noble Books, 2002), 108.

39 Adrian Sargeant and Elaine Jay, Fundraising Management: Analysis, Planning and Practice (New York: Routledge, 2004), 37.

40 Howard W. Olsen and Nancy D. Olsen, Strategic Planning Made Easy for Nonprofit Organizations: A Practical Guide (Reno, NV: M3 Planning, Inc., 2005), 37.

42 These questions are adapted from Olsen and Olsen, 37-38.

43 Aubrey Malphurs, Advanced Strategic Planning: A New Church Model for Church and Ministry Leaders (Grand Rapids: Baker Books, 1999), 152.

44 "Constituent," Merriam-Webster's Collegiate Dictionary, Eleventh Edition: 1998.

45 Jim Henderson and Matt Casper, Jim and Casper Go to Church (Ventura, CA: BarnaBooks, 2007), 96.

46 This is a testimony of an organization that The Vision Group, Ltd., has helped. The names have been changed to protect the individual's privacy.

47 Betty Kirkpatrick, Clichés: Over 1500 Phrases Explored and Explained (New York: St. Martin's Griffin Press, 1999), 160.

48 Gene Logsdon, Gene Logsdon's Money Saving Secrets (Emmaus, PA: Rodale Press, Inc., 1986), 74-75.

49 Covey, The 7 Habits of Highly Effective People: Powerful Lessons in Personal Change, 152.

50 Ibid., 151.

51 Marcus Buckingham and Donald O. Clifton, Now, Discover Your Strengths (New York: Free Press, 2001).

52 Thomas Teal, "The Human Side of Management," in Harvard Business Review on Leadership (Boston: Harvard Business School Press, 1998), 161.

53 Les Daniels and Chip Kidd, Superman: The Complete History (Westminster, MD: Titan Books Ltd, 1998), 19-31.

54 Buckingham and Clifton, 245.

55 Michael E. Hattersley and Linda M. McJannet, Management Communication: Principles and Practice (New York: McGraw-Hill/Irwin, 1997, 2005), 123.

56 Jonathan T. M. Reckford, Opening More Doors: Habitat for Humanity Steps into a New Era (Americus, GA: Habitat for Humanity, 2006), 17.

57 Ibid., 6.

58 Steward and Shook, 210.

59 Keegan, 24.

60 Malphurs, 151ff.

61 G. Richard Shell, Make the Rules or Your Rivals Will (New York: Crown Business, 2004), 267.

62 The list of ten is an adaptation of Chapter 20, "Ten Shortcuts to Getting your Plan Done" in Erica Olsen, Strategic Planning for Dummies (Hoboken, NJ: Wiley Publishing, Inc., 2007), 339-343.

63 Ron Powers, Mark Twain: A Life (New York: Free Press, 2005), 382.

64 Robert Traill, The Jewish War of Flavius Josephus: A New Traslation, vol. 2 (London: Houlston and Stoneman, 1851), 65.

65 Olsen, Strategic Planning for Dummies, 343.

66 Larry the Cable Guy, Git-R-Done (New York: Crown Publishing Group, 2006).

67 Covey, The 7 Habits of Highly Effective People: Powerful Lessons in Personal Change, 195.

68 John Hunt, The Ascent of Everest (Seattle: The Mountaineers Books, 1993), 19.

69 Nancy D. Olsen and Howard W. Olsen, Why Work? Called to Make a Difference (Reno, NV: M3 Planning, Inc., 2006), 130.

70 Collins.